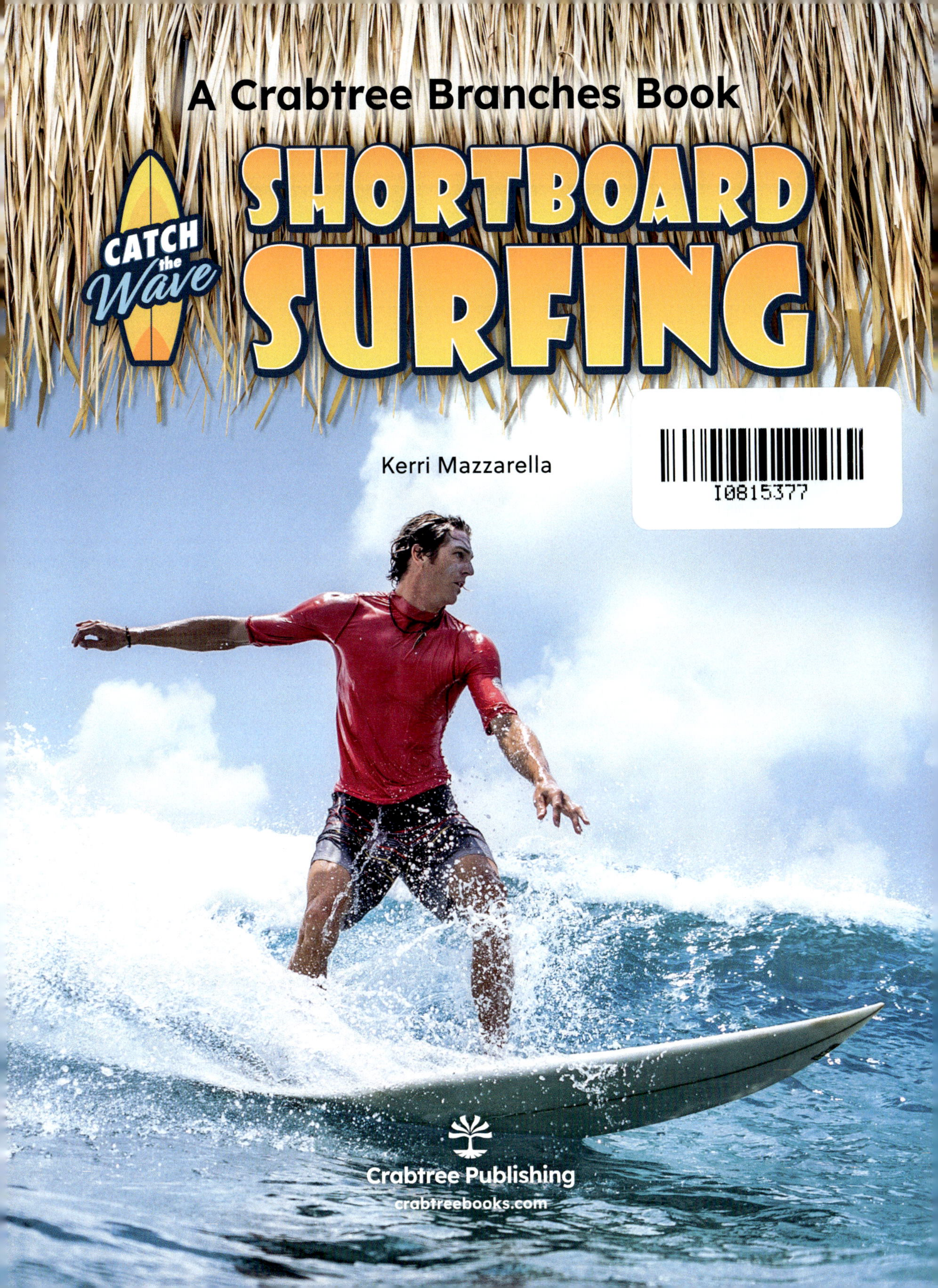

A Crabtree Branches Book
CATCH the Wave
SHORTBOARD SURFING
Kerri Mazzarella
I0815377
Crabtree Publishing
crabtreebooks.com

School-to-Home Support for Caregivers and Teachers

This high-interest book is designed to motivate striving students with engaging topics while building fluency, vocabulary, and an interest in reading. Here are a few questions and activities to help the reader build upon his or her comprehension skills.

Before Reading:

- *What do I think this book is about?*
- *What do I know about this topic?*
- *What do I want to learn about this topic?*
- *Why am I reading this book?*

During Reading:

- *I wonder why...*
- *I'm curious to know...*
- *How is this like something I already know?*
- *What have I learned so far?*

After Reading:

- *What was the author trying to teach me?*
- *What are some details?*
- *How did the photographs and captions help me understand more?*
- *Read the book again and look for the vocabulary words.*
- *What questions do I still have?*

Extension Activities:

- *What was your favorite part of the book? Write a paragraph on it.*
- *Draw a picture of your favorite thing you learned from the book.*

Table of Contents

WHAT IS SHORTBOARD SURFING?

Surfing is the art of balancing on a surfboard and riding waves. In the late 1960s, shortboard surfing evolved, or developed, from the laid-back style of longboard surfing.

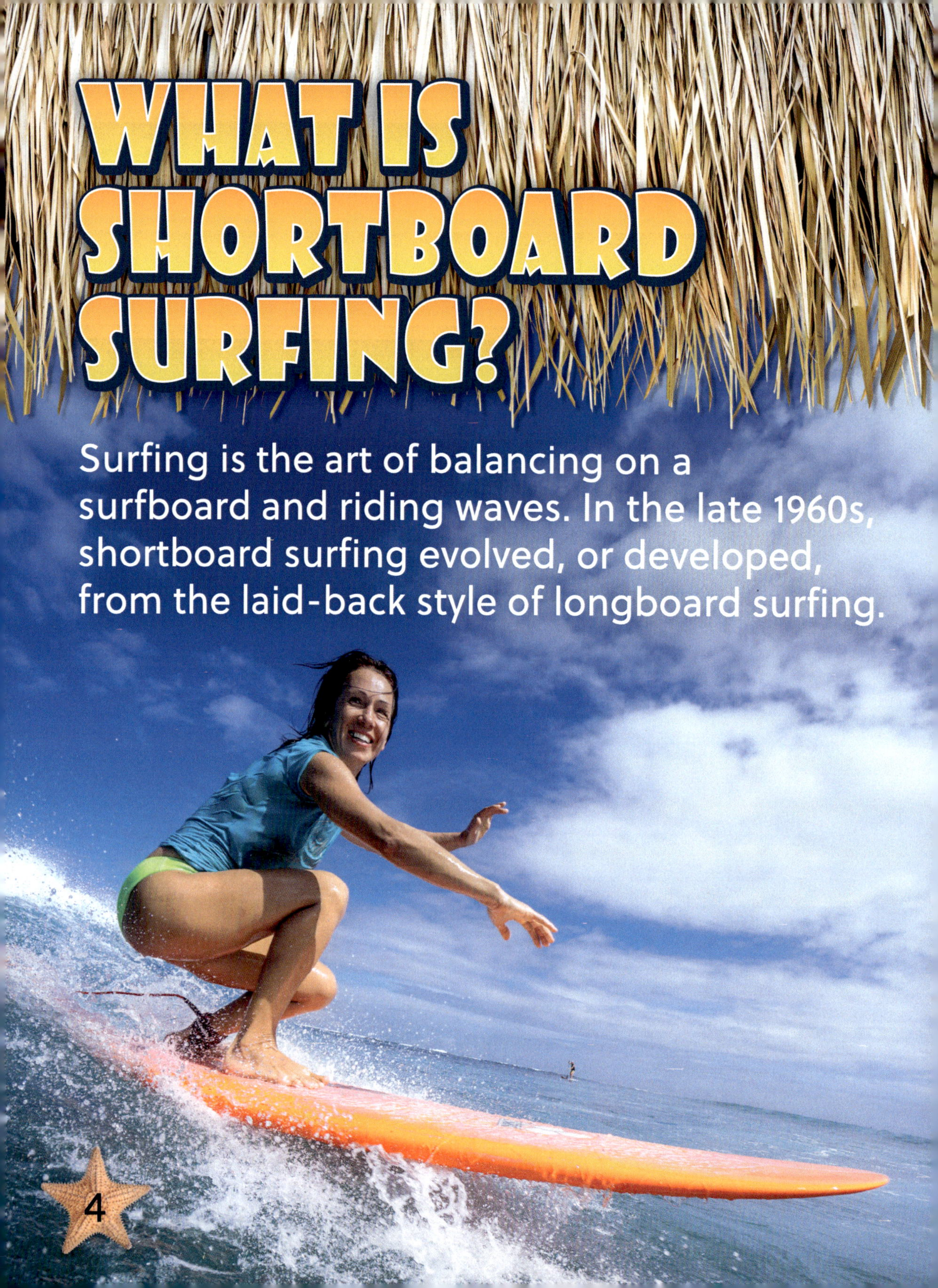

Longboards are surfboards that measure at least 8 feet (2.4 m) in length. Shortboards measure under 7 feet (2.1 m), making them easier to **maneuver** on the wave.

Shortboard surfing introduced complex tricks, tight turns, and moves in the air to the sport of surfing.

Millions of surfers around the world surf on a shortboard for fun. Thousands surf competitively and dream of being a professional surfer one day.

Fact

Becoming a professional, or pro, surfer is very challenging. Pro surfers get paid by winning contests and being **sponsored** by surfing companies.

WHO CAN SHORTBOARD SURF?

Shortboard surfing is not for everyone. Before trying a shortboard, a surfer should master how to ride a longboard.

Shortboards are less **buoyant** than longboards. This makes them more difficult for most beginners to ride.

All kinds of people can enjoy surfing. But a shortboard surfer needs to be physically fit, with excellent **balance**.

Fact

Kelly Slater, one of the most famous surfers in the world, began surfing at the age of five.

CHOOSING YOUR EQUIPMENT

Fact

Custom boards can be specifically designed based on a surfer's ability level, height, and weight. The average cost of a shortboard is $600 to $800.

The most essential piece of equipment you will need is a surfboard. It will be important to choose one that fits you best.

Surf fins are another important piece of equipment. There are many different styles and setups of surf fins. Each is designed for practicing different skills.

surf fins $60–250

You will also need a leash, surf wax, **traction pad**, and a **rash guard**.

Fact

If the water is really cold, you might need to wear a **wetsuit**, booties, and gloves to stay warm.

WHERE TO SHORTBOARD SURF

Shortboard surfing can be done all over the world. Shortboards work well in stronger waves because they are more easily maneuvered than longboards.

Fact

A breaking wave is a wave that crashes over itself at its highest point, called the crest. A surf break is a popular spot where people surf on breaking waves.

Fact

Pipeline, in Hawaii, is one of the most popular surf breaks in the world. California is also home to many epic surf spots. Cocoa Beach, in Florida, is where Kelly Slater first started surfing.

Florida, California, and Hawaii all have countless beaches that are great for surfing in the U.S.

Surfers who are new to shortboard surfing should stay away from rocky beaches, **reefs**, and crowded areas.

HOW TO SHORTBOARD SURF

Surfing a shortboard takes lots of practice. Only skilled surfers can perform tricks such as a barrel ride, a cut back, or an "off the lip."

off the lip

barrel ride

cut back

For some people, shortboard surfing is an activity just for fun. For others, it is a highly competitive sport.

Fact

Most competitive surfers have a coach and train every day.

Every surfer should know some basic rules before paddling out. The surfer closest to the crest of the wave always has the right of way. That means they get to choose whether to ride the wave. Any other surfers in the water must wait their turn.

Surfer's Code

- Do not drop in on, or start to ride, another surfer's wave.
- Do not cut in line to take another surfer's wave.
- Do not let go of your board when a wave is coming toward you.
- Do not be disrespectful to other surfers.

FOR YOUR SAFETY

Any type of surfing can be risky if you are not prepared. Wearing a leash is very important because it keeps your surfboard from floating away and hitting other surfers.

Fact

Around 55 percent of surf injuries are caused by a surfboard.

Fact

Surfers can get surf reports from websites such as Surfline. A surf report gives information about the waves and weather.

It is important to check the surf report for your area. Knowing the weather, sea conditions, and what to do if you are caught in a **rip current** can help keep you safe.

Being aware of your surroundings is important for safety. Reefs, rocks, other surfers, and wildlife are all potential hazards to a surfer.

Fact

Wildlife to watch out for might include stingrays, jellyfish, sharks, and crocodiles. Always leave the water if you see wildlife that could cause you harm.

FAMOUS SHORTBOARD SURFERS

Kelly Slater

Kelly Slater is considered to be one of the greatest surfers of all time. He has won 11 World Titles, 8 Pipe Master Events, and countless other championships over his surfing career.

Fact

The World Surf League (WSL) holds a series of international competitions each year to determine the best male and female surfers in the world.

Fact

Soul Surfer is a movie about surfer Bethany Hamilton. Though she lost her arm at age 13 after being bitten by a shark, she still reached her dream of becoming a professional surfer.

Bethany Hamilton

Andy Irons

Men's champion shortboard surfers include John John Florence, Gabriel Medina, and Andy Irons. Famous female shortboard surfers are Stephanie Gilmore, Lisa Anderson, and Bethany Hamilton.

RESPECTING OUR OCEANS

Oceans make up more than 70 percent of Earth's surface. They provide many benefits to all living things and should be protected.

Fact

The ocean generates over half the oxygen we breathe. Millions of people all over the planet depend on the ocean as their main food source.

One of the biggest threats to our oceans is **pollution**. Surfers can show respect for the ocean by always cleaning up after themselves at the beach and using ocean-safe products, such as sunscreen.

Fact

Surfers started 4Ocean and Surfrider Foundation, organizations dedicated to protecting beaches and oceans worldwide.

Part of respecting the ocean as a surfer is knowing how to stay safe. The ocean is beautiful, but the power of the waves can be dangerous if you are not careful.

Shortboard surfing is one of the most popular types of surfing. It is also the most competitive. With some hard work and dedication, maybe you could become a surfing champion!

Glossary

balance (bal-uhns): Your ability to remain steady and upright

buoyant (boi-ent): Able to stay afloat

maneuver (muh-noo-ver): To move with skill and care

pollution (puh-loo-shuhn): Harmful materials that damage or contaminate the air, water, and soil

rash guard (rash-gahrd): A fitted shirt worn while surfing to protect the skin from the Sun and from rough surfaces

reefs (reefs): Strips of rock, sand, or coral close to the surface of the ocean

rip current (rip-kur-uhnt): A strong flow of water running from a beach back to the open ocean

sponsored (spon-serd): Received money in return for promoting a company or brand

traction pad (trak-shuhn pad): A pad that sticks to a surfboard to help keep the surfer from slipping

wetsuit (wet-soot): A close-fitting suit, usually made of a type of rubber called neoprene, that is worn in cold water to retain body heat

Index

Websites to Visit

https://www.redbull.com/us-en/shortboard-vs-longboard-surfing

https://bethanyhamilton.com/biography

https://www.surfertoday.com/surfing/the-surfing-equipment-list

https://www.surfinghandbook.com/knowledge/ocean-safety/

About the Author

Kerri Mazzarella was raised on the East Coast of southern Florida. Living near the beach has given her the opportunity to watch all types of surfing throughout her life. All four of her children have done their fair share of bodysurfing over the years for fun! Surfing is a great way to connect with the ocean and get some exercise. Her youngest son is a competitive shortboard surfer and travels all over the world to surf!

Written by: Kerri Mazzarella
Designed by: Bobbie Houser
Series Development: James Earley
Proofreader: Janine Deschenes
Educational Consultant: Marie Lemke M.Ed.

Photographs:
t = Top, c = Center, b = Bottom, l = Left, r = Right

Alamy: Manuel Balesteri: p. 8; paul kennedy: p. 27

Shutterstock: Dudarev Mikhail: cover, p. 1; ohrim: p. 4; EpicStockMedia: p. 5; Yuri Dondish: p. 6; William. Visuals: p. 7; Dane Gillett: p. 8; RugliG: p. 9; Denis Moskvinov: p. 10; KIRAYONAK YULIYA: p. 11; jakkapan: p. 12 t; nvphoto: p. 12 bl; Dogora Sun: p. 12 br; Photo Volcano: p. 13 tl; dreii: p. 13 tc, lc; Rawpixel.com: p. 13 tr; Iakovleva Daria: p. 13 bl; Lilkin: p. 13 br; JJM Photography: p. 14; Michael Hillman: p. 15, 28-29; ENeems: p. 16; RovingPhotogZA: p. 17 tr; Lila Koan: p. 17 bl; Nick Donaghy: p. 17 br; Judith Lienert: p. 19; Simone Hogan: p. 20; Anatoliy Tesouro: p. 22; Mitroshenkov Ilia: p. 23; homydesign: p. 24; Brian A. Witkin: p. 25 t; jarvis gray: p. 25 b; Rich Carey: p. 26

Crabtree Publishing

crabtreebooks.com 800-387-7650

Printed in the U.S.A./052025/CP20250422

Published in Canada
Crabtree Publishing
616 Welland Ave.
St. Catharines, Ontario
L2M 5V6

Published in the United States
Crabtree Publishing
347 Fifth Ave
Suite 1402-145
New York, NY 10016

Library and Archives Canada Cataloguing in Publication
Available at Library and Archives Canada

Library of Congress Cataloging-in-Publication Data
Available at the Library of Congress

Hardcover: 978-1-0398-8026-9
Paperback: 978-1-0398-8386-4
Ebook (pdf): 978-1-0398-8146-4
Epub: 978-1-0398-8266-9